THE AMERICAN VISION

THE AMERICAN VISION

AN ESSAY ON THE FUTURE OF DEMOCRATIC CAPITALISM

MICHAEL NOVAK

American Enterprise Institute for Public Policy Research
Washington, D.C.

Michael Novak is the Ledden-Watson Distinguished Professor of Religion at Syracuse University (on leave) and a resident scholar at the American Enterprise Institute.

Note: An earlier version of this paper was written at Syracuse University on a consultantship to the Exxon Corporation. Both the author and the American Enterprise Institute are grateful to the Exxon Corporation for the right to reproduce it. Responsibility for the opinions expressed in it rests solely with the author.

ISBN 0–8447–3324–5

AEI studies 222

Library of Congress Catalog Card No. 78–23794

Printed in the United States of America

CONTENTS

PART TWO
Strategies

1

Introduction

Bernard-Henri Levy, one of the "new philosophers" of France, while revolted by Marxism, nourishes a typical view of democratic capitalism: "Capitalism says: men are pure things, abstract and equivalent, measured by their exchange value, in an infernal world that deprives and diminishes them." [1] But this, of course, is not what a democratic capitalist society is about at all. One can see how M. Levy might have seized upon certain sentences in Adam Smith, Ayn Rand, or Milton Friedman as a justification for his accusation. The theoreticians of our system do make it sound more crass in theory than it actually is in practice. Indeed, we do not actually have a theory that expresses our vision of the good and just society. There is no single book one would willingly place in the hands of a serious inquirer and say: "Here is our full moral, political, and economic vision." Granted that our system is complex, and granted that it is pluralistic, encompassing many metaphysical and cultural visions rather than one alone; still, it is, to say the least, awkward that we have no overarching vision to express, no electrifying text to send into the worldwide ideological battle in which we are engaged.

One reason for this deficiency is that our system is a trinitarian system. It is three systems in one. It is, at once, an economic system, a political system, and a cultural system. If any one of these is injured, the others are injured, too. If any one is missing, the resulting system falls short of our dreams.

Since our system is tripartite, specialists often miss its essence; each gets only part of it. The economists, the political theorists, the humanists each miss too much. Still, it should be possible, one imagines, to articulate our dream—all of it.

---

[1] Bernard-Henri Levy, *The New Republic*, February 11, 1978.

1

I propose to attempt this articulation in several stages. The essential method is to think concretely, staying quite close to actual experiences we all share. The air is already thick with ideology. The several factions seem to be shooting past each other. Writers talk about a "capitalism" and a "socialism" made of frozen blocks of theory. They seek out hidden "contradictions" in the logic and structure of each opposing system. But in fact we do not live in theories but in real, concrete systems. Since World War II, we have gained sufficient evidence to be able to argue in a down-to-earth and experiential way; the number of both capitalist and socialist systems has multiplied. Many aspects of our experience have never been articulated in any theory. There are many surprises, many paradoxes, many things that "shouldn't" be as they actually are. Since each of us has only one life to live, and not an excessive amount of time for sorting out the endless complexities of rival theories, it seems entirely appropriate, and even a matter of a certain sort of intellectual integrity, to hold fast to the evidence of one's own actual experiences, even in the face of theoreticians who tell us what we "ought" to think. Clear thinking accepts no loyalty tests, except to the evidence of its own experience and its own standards of judgment.

In thinking about "our own experience," we are bound to think historically about our own families. In the year 1900, over half of all Americans were living below the level of subsistence. In 1932, the families of many of those who are now the writers, intellectuals, and business and civic leaders of the nation experienced bitter poverty. Most of the persons I have worked with professionally over the years are of such families. In speaking about "systems," we cannot help noting what the system into which our families were inserted—often fewer than one hundred years ago—has made possible. We do not imagine that there is, or can be, a perfect social system. Systems are relative. Any American can compare his or her lot now, however, with the lot of others of like class in their country of origin. This is true of Africans and Asians, Latin Americans, and Europeans. The United States is not now, and never has been, a nation of full justice, equality, fraternity, or opportunity. It has often been harsh and unfair. But compared with what? One may be quite cleareyed about the inadequacies of our system. One must be equally cleareyed about its relative performance.

Some writers are intimidated by the charge that they are "middle-class intellectuals," and do not speak for the poor of America or of the Third World. The very notion that whole populations may be upwardly mobile, and that free persons might speak freely and ac-

2

curately about their own circumstances, is not universal in human experience. Intellectuals here continue to rise out of the ranks of the poor. How faithfully intellectuals continue to maintain contact with their own origins is part of the theme of this paper.

My proposal, then, is to proceed by small steps. First I would like to consider some of the advantages, as they appear to me, of having been nourished in a democratic capitalist system; next, some of the disadvantages of same, and some of the reasons why socialism exerts so powerful an attraction upon the mind and heart. Thirdly, I analyze the emergence of a new adversarial class in American society and the reasons—buried deep in its own intellectual history, and even more so in its present political and economic interests— why an influential portion of this new class is so determined in its opposition to the business class and so hostile to the project of democratic capitalism. Finally, I return to the task of looking at our own system with fresh eyes, as far as possible escaping the blinders of available theories, and attempting to see our actual experiences straight. In Part Two, I offer strategies which the leaders of the democratic capitalist system might follow in the war of ideas with its adversaries.

There are ideals within our system which we seldom articulate. These ideals, which spring up from within our system, are transcendent. They enable us to criticize our system quite effectively. In order to be critical and cleareyed, it is not necessary to go outside our system. Most critics of our system, however, scandalized by certain of its deficiencies, conventionally turn to socialism. For reasons to be enumerated below, this turn to socialism is intellectually self-defeating. Socialism is no longer a dream or a vision to be found only in books; some fourscore or more nations have built themselves firmly upon its ideals. One can now, as one could not thirty years ago, study socialism as it actually functions in actual experience and practice. The results do not accord with expectations.

PART ONE
The War of Ideas

2
Democratic Capitalism
Briefly Considered

I designate our system by the name "democratic capitalism" in order to stress its tripartite nature. It is not an *economic* system only, but a *political* and *cultural* system as well. The name "democratic capitalism" suggests clearly the political and the economic structure of our ideals. It suggests as well, although less directly, a commitment to those cultural ideals that might be expressed by some such locution as "a liberal civilization"—a civilization whose aims include an open society, respect for the rights and dignity of individuals, and the vision of justice and equity that has been developing in Western society since earliest times.

Ours is *not* a system of "free enterprise" only, nor of "private property," nor of "individual liberties," nor of "limited government" alone. These are locutions proper to a preoccupation with the economic sphere, and they seem to be favored by writers and speakers whose interests are mainly those of economics and business. They will not suffice as descriptions of our system as a whole, as it actually is experienced. They will not command the full loyalties, nor express the full interests, of all who enjoy the fruits of our system. Thus, most available defenses of our system spring from a base too narrow both in the interests to which they appeal and in the intellectual grounds on which they stand. The designation "democratic capitalism" is intended to go beyond a description of the economic system merely, and to include the political system and the cultural system, too.

Strengths of Democratic Capitalism

Many of the critics of democratic capitalism discuss its economic system wholly in terms of its alleged "expropriation" and "pollution" of nature's resources. Yet Marx held that the capitalist stage was

7

essential to the emergence of socialism, because it alone could enrich the world and build an economic base for a vision of plenty. In a world of inevitable scarcity, equality is not imaginable. Only in a world of plenty can there emerge a vision of equal distribution, with enough of everything for everyone.

More to the point, the emergence of democratic capitalism did not take place everywhere in the world at once. As a system of economic organization, it was invented rather late in human history and, at first, only in a few centers of activity: in Great Britain, in Flanders, in Germany—in short, in northwestern Europe. This late emergence led Max Weber to speculate upon the importance to the development of the capitalist idea of Protestant (especially Calvinist) culture. Not only was culture significant from the first; so also was politics. The development of capitalism in economics was accompanied in a few places by the emergence of democracy in politics. In a few nations, economic habits and political habits reinforced one another in the daily practices of citizens. From the beginning, then, the trinitarian and interdependent nature of the system—the concomitant development of economic, political, and cultural ideals—has been in evidence.

Capitalism and Wealth. Those who have experienced the growing power of this tripartite system have experienced the first of its often overlooked advantages: its *wealth-conferring* character. The earth has long been rich in oil, copper, iron ore, rubber, and countless other resources. But for millennia, many of these resources went unknown, neglected, or unused. The imagination and enterprise unleashed by democratic capitalism brought recognition of the actual wealth lying fallow in the bosom of nature; invented new uses for these resources; and conferred wealth on many regions of the world that the inhabitants of those regions did not know they possessed. As an instance, consider how oil lay unknown and unused under the deserts of Araby. Only with the development of the piston engine was a use for that heretofore useless stuff invented.

Many of us saw evidence of the wealth-conferring nature of our system during the bicentennial celebrations in many American towns and cities in 1976. At the turn of the century, in the year 1900, most of America shared a poverty normal to humankind. In bicentennial parades, one watched the implements, tools, and artifacts of preceding generations pass by on floats. In towns in Iowa (themselves barely a century old), one saw vividly that within the lifetimes of our own grandparents the United States was what we would now call an "underdeveloped country." Farm implements were made of wood and the most primitive ores; power came through the muscles of men and animals. The laws of erosion and crop rotation, of soil and water management, and other scientific agricultural skills were then largely unknown. The rise of democratic capitalism conferred enormous wealth upon the citizens of such towns within some seventy-six years, a very short period in human history.

Efficiencies. If democratic capitalism has conferred enormous wealth upon the world, a wealth never before even envisaged except in a few places, for a very few, and unsteadily, it has also proven to be the most *efficient* system ever devised by human beings. Whatever its faults—and these are many—no other system even comes close to it in inventiveness, production, and widespread distribution. Socialist systems have proved to be less successful. (Since the Communist Revolution of 1917, the Soviet Union, once capable of being the breadbasket of large sections of the world, has had sixty years of "poor weather.") It is not necessary to make this point invidiously. There are serious flaws in the sort of efficiency generated by democratic capitalism. Unplanned and unguided, our system permits shortages in some areas and unnecessary abundance and wastage in others, until the market corrects them; and in some areas the market does not work well. But the very idea that plenty is attainable— that there might be a material abundance to be equitably distributed— is singularly founded upon the enormous wealth produced by such a system.

Capitalism and Democracy. There is a third advantage gained by a democratic capitalist system, an advantage that looks to the political rather than to the economic sphere. Capitalism may flourish without democracy, but democracy apart from capitalism is very difficult to achieve. Between capitalism and democracy there is an underlying system of mutual reinforcement, an internal harmony. There are examples of welfare states (they are more properly called socialist), that are democratic—Great Britain, Sweden, Israel, among others. But in all of these, underlying traditions owe much to a liberal capitalist past. Those nations that have leaped straight into socialism, which they insist upon describing as "democratic," manifest strong centralized governments, without checks and balances, and deficient institutions for the defense of individual rights. Traditions of private property and individual rights grew up in the capitalist orbit. An economic order built upon respect for the decisions of the individual in the marketplace; upon rights to property which the state may not abridge; and upon limiting the activities of the central state, are at the very least harmonious with the habits of mind required for a functioning democratic political order.

There are several examples in recent history of capitalist authoritarian regimes moving in the direction of a democratic political order. There are no examples of socialist regimes doing so. In theory, perhaps, there is no contradiction between democracy and socialism. In practice, clearly there is.

Habits of Mind. My fourth observation concerns the cultural sphere. Democratic capitalism depends upon a unique human type. Three habits of mind, in particular, must be highly developed if democratic capitalism is to function. These habits of mind are not wholly virtuous; they include, as we will shortly notice, certain important deficiencies. They are, nevertheless, both distinctive and admirable. They represent three forms of spiritual enrichment uniquely available in our culture.

• The first of these is an *empirical* habit of mind. Whatever the traditional way of doing things, whatever the conventions, whatever the prevailing theories, the system of democratic capitalism rewards a systematic skepticism and a basic trust in experience. It encourages citizens to invent new ways better in tune with experience. Our culture teaches us to be heedless of theory and to look with fresh eyes at the facts. In one sense, of course, the suggestion box found so often in factories and schools is an invitation to theoretical thinking, to imagination, to ideas. But what it teaches, above all, is that we should keep our eyes upon our own experiences, that we should be taught by what we actually encounter rather than by what someone else laid down from a distance. My father-in-law, a lawyer from Iowa, used to instruct me: "Michael, if you can't do it, teach it." Priority is given to the man of action; the man of theory is viewed with a certain skepticism. This empirical habit of mind, despite obvious weaknesses, is a source of considerable intellectual and cultural power.

• The second habit of mind is related to the first: It is the habit of *pragmatism*. No matter what theories may dictate, this habit of mind instructs us to observe: *How does it work in practice?* Our culture encourages a pervasive recognition of the limits of theory and of the intractability of the real world. We have trained ourselves to find intellectual excitement in the task of solving concrete problems. By contrast, the solution of conceptual puzzles seems rather like a form of diversion. In the academic world, many of the most promising intellects soon find greater satisfaction in the challenges of administration than at their tame and safely protected desks.

Our businessmen prize doing rather than theorizing. They are, by and large, indifferent to the need to conceptualize their tasks, to theorize about them, or to get straight all the ideological implications of what they do. They would rather build a plant for Pepsi Cola or Ford in Leningrad than argue with party·apparatchiks about the relative merits of capitalism. They seem to believe that if only they build a better mousetrap, the world will come to their door. It is not necessary to succeed on the plane of theory, they hold, if one can excel every day in the realm of practice. In these days, of course, the side made to seem attractive in the media can ride roughshod over facts, experience, and reality. Pragmatism is not enough. But it has its clear rewards.

Marx wrote that changing the world is more important than understanding it correctly. In this light, the pragmatism of our civilization may come to seem more highly developed than that of the Marxist world. Our pragmatists, at least, are not burdened by the official blinders of the Marxist state and party apparatus. They travel with so much less ideological baggage that Schumpeter was led to theorize that they might in the long run prove spineless against the onslaught upon them by a more theoretical and principled socialism. So our pragmatism hurts us both by depriving us of an ideological offensive, and by leaving us weaponless in defense.

• The third habit of mind nourished in our civilization is the habit of *practical compromise*. In order to sign a commercial contract, or in order to pass a bill through our legislatures, we do not consider it necessary to reach agreement on all the metaphysical, religious, or intellectual implications that may be involved. We train ourselves to be rather studiously nonideological and "nonprincipled," and to accept the best concrete compromise we can attain. We try not to insist upon total ideological harmony. We agree to disagree, even while signing on the dotted line to provide the specified limited services. In order to accomplish something, we have been well tutored, it is not necessary to agree about everything.

The world of action is not the same as the world of faith, or vision, or theory, or ideal. Our vision of history is not, in that sense, simple or absolutist. We recognize that different parties may cherish different visions, and that our opponents, rather than we, may perhaps in the long run prove to be correct. We are satisfied with modest incremental steps forward. This willingness to compromise is one of the main propellants of this nation's social dynamism. More romantic persons, who insist upon pure devotion to their own clear ideals, strike us as quixotic and, in the end, self-destructive. We half admire them, but we do not believe that history works as they seem to assume. We are rather systematically modest about the capacity of systems of ideals to match the real complexities of history. Almost uniquely among the peoples of the world, we prefer to be tutored slowly by actual experience, step by step, experiment by experiment. This intellectual modesty, this willingness to compromise, is a national strength. But it, too, has its own inherent dangers and flaws.

Disadvantages of Democratic Capitalism

Indeed, if the four points just enumerated convey some of the chief strengths of democratic capitalism, the habits of mind the system encourages convey as well some of its serious disadvantages. First, a concentration upon the empirical and the pragmatic tends, after a while, to impoverish the human spirit. For the human being learns in time that even the greatest empirical success in bringing about desired outcomes does not satisfy the human heart. The meaning of life is not satisfied solely by accomplishments in managing the world. Achieving these, the soul still hungers for love, community, justice, and the attainment of moral ideals, and seeks the satisfactions of the arts, leisure well spent among loved ones, family life, and interior adventures of the spirit. Precisely on these grounds, many successful men and women today are dissatisfied with their lives. Concentration upon the empirical and the pragmatic makes the practitioners of democratic capitalism effective and powerful; it does not make them noble, virtuous, or happy. In an ironic way, the very successes of democratic capitalism lay it open to the charge of spiritual poverty. The habit of evading questions of "meaning" in order to concentrate upon what may be done in the world of fact renders the human person disappointed, in the end, with his or her own performance. The hunger for "meaning" is spoken of with longing by many successful persons today.

Second, the habit of seeking a practical compromise is a significant moral and social strength. But it, too, may leave the spirit unhappy about not having cleaved to inwardly nourishing ideals.

Third, the system in which we live prides itself upon identifying and satisfying the desires of a maximum number of persons. It does so, democratically, in the marketplace. No matter what elitists may say the people "should" want, the desires actually expressed in the marketplace are the ones business rushes to fill (as do the politicians and, indeed, the makers of culture). Yet the very process of appealing to wants and desires has the paradoxical effect of undermining certain disciplines essential to democratic capitalism. Only a culture in which a majority of citizens is capable of deferred gratification, of a sense of responsibility, and of a capacity for saving and wise investment, can support a democratic political system and a capitalist economic system. By concentrating upon fulfilling desires, democratic capitalism nourishes a hedonism which undermines the self-denying spirit. Competition to satisfy desires drives out appeals to restraint, discipline, and responsibility. Political leaders who promise benefits while exacting few costs win popular support; so do the makers of culture and business enterprises alike. Ironically, then, the success of the system in satisfying wider and wider ranges of desire results in a weakening of the system.

Fourth, the appeal of democratic capitalism to the self-interest of each individual, while modified by multiple appeals to the spirit of fraternity, cooperation, and generosity, nevertheless heightens the impression made by the system as a whole that it is based on a radical form of selfishness. The inevitable result of such a system, some conclude, is a pattern of shocking inequalities. Democratic capitalism was in the mind of its first theoreticians a marvelously designed method for harnessing the energies of human self-interest and selfishness for social purposes. There seems to be no question that this design has been successful. The explosion of human inventiveness and enterprise which it nourished is historically unprecedented. The face of the earth has been changed. The social and communal benefits of the system are manifest. Yet, a suspicion remains that the entire design is vaguely immoral; that it yields too much to human selfishness; that it encourages the worst in the human breast. The articulation of the ideals of democracy and capitalism has perhaps erred on the side of exalting the individual and, specifically, the selfish instincts of the individual, at the expense of human sociality. On balance, the actual practice of our system is probably superior to our way of describing it. Still this objection is telling.

Finally, the strength of the business community and of its intellectual specialists in concentrating upon the practical order carries with it profound weakness in the fields of theory and ideology. This weakness has become glaring in an age of mass communications, in which political, economic, and cultural matters are contested in instant and vivid symbols. A system highly successful in practice may be perceived in symbol and ideology to be inferior. Perceptions may be stronger than reality. In the highly technological culture of the post-war era, the rules of ideological warfare have been changed. The field of conflict has moved into the sphere of communications and ideas and symbols. Such matters move people. They have a tremendous effect upon both political systems and markets. It is not enough, these days, to build a better mousetrap. A shift in ideas or symbols may make mousetraps seem obsolete or even perhaps objects of loathing.

Thus, the fact that democratic capitalism is wealth-conferring and efficient beyond all other systems in meeting popular needs may count for less than it should in the world of theory, ideology, and propaganda. To an enormous extent, the balance of power in world affairs is now decided in the realm of ideas and symbols. Precisely here the perennial strengths of democratic capitalism in empiricism and pragmatism have become a serious cultural weakness. There is no "Capitalist Manifesto," no sense of the "manifest destiny" in liberal civilization. Our myths may no longer move millions as do the myths of socialism.

In the sphere of ideology and ideas, among the artists and intellectuals, as well as among the masses of the world's people, the advantages at present seem clearly to belong to the opponents of democratic capitalism. To a remarkable extent, this seems to be true among many intellectuals within the civilization of democratic capitalism itself.

3

The Attractions of Socialism

Socialism exerts powerful attractions upon many. In 1957, after a lecture to a group of students, the eminent theologian Paul Tillich replied to a question about whether he still supported socialism. The reply came quickly: "That is the only possible economic system from the Christian point of view." [1] There are several features of socialism that attract such support.

Brotherhood. Socialism presents a vision of human brotherhood, whereas the classics of capitalism stress the individual and enlightened egotism. The classics of socialism make those who read them glow with a sense of human solidarity. This is a profoundly religious and humanistic motivation. It nourishes the spirit even in dry times.

A Moral Vision. Socialism presents an inherently moral vision, describing a "new man" and "new woman" who will be nourished under a new type of social order. The classic writings of socialism are scathing in their criticisms of the moral flaws found so abundantly in the real world of existing social orders (at that time, capitalist social orders). These classic writings then describe the contours of the coming and ardently desired future society in almost wholly moral terms: a society of brotherliness, freedom, equality, dignity, and creativity, and an end to alienation and isolation. Socialism is not only a political and social system; it represents as well a moral vision. Its appeal is quite religious. By contrast, the classics of capitalism commonly leave religion to the archbishops, so to speak, and leave moral striving to the individual. It is as though democratic

---

[1] J. Phillip Wogaman recounts this episode in *The Great Economic Debate*, (Philadelphia: The Westminster Press, 1977), p. 133.

capitalist writers leave the articulation of society's moral vision to others, whereas socialist writers, distrusting other sources on the question, pour a high proportion of their energy into describing the moral quality and moral consequences of their vision.

A Theory of History. Socialism offers a theory of history. In the socialist view, human history has a hidden meaning and a clear direction. The name of its goal is socialism. It is a comforting feeling to be on the side of history; to feel that one is in tune, so to speak, with the universe, to sense that all one's efforts—even those that fail and are broken—are redeemed by being on the side of inexorable progressive forces.

An Ontology. Socialism also offers an ontology, a theory by which to determine what is real and what is illusory, what has "being" and what is only "appearance." Things may be true but not really important, because they are bound to fade away. Thus, for example, the overwhelming power of capitalism and its successes are treated as though they were part of a mirage, a system tottering on weak foundations, a reality that is doomed to pass away and, therefore, not nearly as substantial as it seems. When a democratic capitalist and a socialist are in conversation, it is often as if they are perceiving two different realities. What one finds hard fact, the other dismisses as illusory or insignificant. What one finds hopeful, the other finds trivial and misleading. Thus socialists regularly predict (as Michael Harrington recently has) the "twilight of capitalism." Thus, too, many socialists must have gained confirmation for their own sense of reality from the sudden collapse of the overwhelming U.S. military might in Vietnam, precisely in the fashion Ho Chi Minh had long before predicted.

Symbolism. Finally, socialism affords the mythic and symbolic mind many graphic symbols of good and evil. Images of dollar signs, profits, tycoons, moneybags, and round-stomached, dandily dressed capitalists express an almost tangible sense of evil. Images of aspiration among the poor and the oppressed, images of smiles upon the faces of the worker (perhaps through streaming tears) and willful courage, images of ordinary people striving upwards and perhaps rebelliously, a rifle in one hand and a plough in the other, represent the good. Socialism has captured many, although not all, of the images of the frontier. It is able to appeal to existing abuses,

16

corruptions, evils, and wrongs, on the negative side, and to images of upward struggle on the other.

Democratic capitalists believe so strongly in human freedom and its ambiguities that they may be reluctant to promise moral goodness. They tend to offer images of rising standards of living, wealth, opportunity, and liberty, but not of moral striving. Socialists portray their partisans as morally superior, saintly, compassionate, and humanistic. To be sure, Western habits of skepticism and criticism lead to the debunking of Western heroes; whereas socialist states, unfettered by the critical instinct, glorify their own. Even independently of the machinery of glorification, however, socialism portrays the essential human struggle as a moral one, while democratic capitalism abandons that field to the theologians, the preachers, and the humanists: maintains, one might say, a modest silence.

4

The Cultural System of Democratic Capitalism

The attacks upon democratic capitalism come from so many directions that it is difficult to reply to them one by one. Besides, most attacks come from so pervasive a conviction that capitalism is the root of all evils that replying to them one by one seldom really satisfies its critics. Still, many drift into anticapitalist sentiments through the mere repetition of individual criticisms. Thus, in fighting what is mainly an intellectual struggle, one must fight on many fronts at once. Intellectual arguments are seldom won by one brilliant thrust; usually they are won when the opposition's arguments begin to weaken along a whole range of issues. The best defense is, then, a good offense. The best offensive thrust available to democratic capitalism is an aggressive statement of its results in the sphere of culture, and a direct attack upon the assumptions of its principal opponents.

The impact of democratic capitalism upon the sphere of culture is, moreover, the single theme most neglected in the literature. Economists and businessmen worry about the economic aspects of our system, and naively leave the cultural aspects to others. But most cultural thinkers begin from anticapitalist traditions. Thus humanists tend to be antagonistic toward the modern world of commercialism, plastics, instant gratification, and the like, while social scientists tend to concentrate upon the pathologies of capitalism and to champion remote ideals of community and perfect justice. Hardly anyone looks at our actual system as a whole, relating its cultural freedoms to its economic and political freedoms.

We begin, then, in an uncharted area. A useful technique is to take up some central ideals of our tripartite system and to pay attention to the texture of our daily lives rather than to theory. Consider the ideals of *fraternity, equality,* and *liberty.*

Fraternity

We often hear accusations that our system produces loneliness, anomie, selfishness, and competitiveness. The system is described as a "rat race." Yet out of our culture come many remarkable imperatives of *fraternity.* In the actual workings of our daily lives, our system tutors us to many ideals for which it receives too little credit, among them the *spirit of cooperation.* The Soviet defector who flew his MIG to Japan commented upon his experience on the U.S. naval vessel that ferried him to the United States, to the effect that he had never seen crewmen work together harmoniously and without autocratic commands. Teamwork is an attitude our culture nourishes. Our vast social and occupational mobility is made possible by this attitude. Even in a group of relative strangers, Americans are trained to pitch in, to learn the job as they go, to watch others, to adapt themselves to their tasks—in short, to exhibit both personal initiative and a spirit of adaptation to others. In a political campaign, it is often possible for a group of strangers to meet for the first time, to divide tasks, and to work in significant interdependence, under self-direction, and at high intensity, with a minimum of authoritarian supervision. We train our young people to become both self-starters and good team players.

Now this is, according to prevailing theory, quite odd. Our society is supposed to be individualistic. But in actual practice, it is probably superior to socialist systems in engendering high social skills. It does so on several levels at once.

• The cultural system deeply values *associational activities.* The games most loved by our young people—football, baseball, and basketball—are team games, and it is perhaps the achievement of perfect teamwork within them that brings participants their greatest remembered pleasures and their fondest success. Moreover, Americans are great "joiners." "Forming a committee" is our favorite national pastime. John Dewey is the father of our main philosophical contribution to educational theory, and it is precisely the social skills of teamwork and cooperativeness on which he laid maximal stress. A group of Americans at work or at play manifests extraordinary organizational instincts, forming associations or teams for a multiplicity of purposes. No doubt this instinct is as old as the frontier spirit, as barn building and the church socials, and as familiar to all of us as are the bridge club, the block party, the local little league, and the girl scouts. Organizing ourselves for play, for work, and for private or public purposes is one of the salient characteristics of our way of life.

• The cultural system deeply values *the adaptation of self to others*. We encourage children to be sensitive to the needs and demands of the groups in which they participate and to others in those groups. We give "congeniality" awards. We admire persons who remain calm, kindly, courteous, and easy to get along with. The public respect for good team players, regular guys, easygoing bosses, and a folksy and friendly style is easy to mock, but it does represent a great social resource. Severe critics of the personality type developed in our system are sharply critical of our "other-directedness" (David Riesman, *The Lonely Crowd*, 1950) and "conformism" (William H. Whyte, Jr., *The Organization Man*, 1956). But if every virtue has its vice, then such alleged pervasive flaws in the national character point to the strong social ideals promoted in this supposedly individualistic nation.

• The cultural system deeply values *indirect, informal, and democratic forms* of practicing authority. It is true that we still see in our society some models of strong, autocratic forms of exercising authority, in football coaches like Vince Lombardi, in generals like George S. Patton, and in others. But such models have vociferous critics. In most places, the cultural style runs counter to the autocratic manner. The contemporary manager has had to master multiple forms of indirection, informality, and group process, in order to elicit leadership from staff members and other members of the group. We value most strong leaders who give direction but who seem to excel in perceiving just what it is that those they lead wish to do, so that their directions seem to get their pervasive power from the group itself.

• The cultural system deeply values the ideal of *fraternity*. Although we still encounter leaders who are aloof, reclusive, misanthropic, and lacking in any common touch, it has been plain from the beginning that in our culture we are taught to prefer leaders who are "one of us" rather than "above us." The rejection of monarchy was a great symbolic act, issuing in the quite different cultural style of the "republican spirit." This was, in a sense, a rejection of the paternal spirit in favor of the fraternal. It was this symbol that Thomas Jefferson evoked in his eschewing of pomp and circumstance, as did Jimmy Carter in his more recent walk from the Capitol to the White House on Inauguration Day. Not only is it true that millions of Americans voluntarily belong to various fraternal organizations and sororities, dedicated to service to their fellows; it is also true that the model of brotherly or sisterly belonging is the controlling model of nearly all our relationships. Even husbands and wives are expected to be "buddies," and fathers and mothers to be "chums" to their children. Supervisor and boss, professor and editor-in-chief, are expected to exercise the authority of their positions while doing so in a fraternal style. Wilson C. McWilliams in *The Idea of Fraternity in America* (1973) shows how fundamental—and how thoroughly neglected—the brotherly (sisterly) ideal has been in American life.

• The cultural system deeply values in its citizens the ideal of *task-orientation*. In his discussion of the many kinds of love, *Four Loves* (1960), C. S. Lewis remarks that true lovers do not concentrate on looking into each other's eyes but, rather, on goals they seek in common. American youngsters are trained from a very early age to take part in many different sorts of activities in many different groups, and to apply and to withdraw their full attention as they move from one task to another. They are taught to focus upon the task to be done at each place and at each time. So much time for this; so much time for that. All these "time modules" prepare them for life in a mobile, pluralistic society in which they will move freely among multiple possibilities. Very few of them will live in tight, homogeneous communities, where they will share in total community as most persons did, once upon a time. On the contrary, they will choose how to spend their time, usually with different persons for different purposes, at home, at work, and in their leisure time. Most will belong to many different communities and will share all these communities, perhaps, with no other person. For this reason, grounded in the structure of a free and mobile society, our citizens learn almost by second nature to concentrate upon tasks one at a time, and to work as easily as possible with the many different sorts of groups in which they take part. The discovery of an unusually good group, within which we can become excited about an unusually rewarding project, forms the highlight of many of our lives.

Contrary to ideology, then, a democratic capitalist society like ours develops a very high degree of sociality in its citizens. It may well be true that no society in history has ever surpassed ours in the type, degree, range, or power of the social habits it nourishes. Our military men pride themselves upon the capacity of each unit—

even under stress and even when its official leaders have been lost—to think and act for itself, to improvise, and to survive by its social skills. Our corporate and economic life depends heavily upon being able to take these skills for granted. (Indeed, populations in which these skills are less highly developed may have special problems finding or holding employment precisely on these grounds.) Our political parties, campaigns, and ad hoc organizations are inconceivable without this enormous fund of skills distributed broadly throughout the population.

Why, then, is our system not praised for its superior fulfillment of the idea of *fraternity?* Ideologically based objections to our alleged rampant individualism, like the frequently heard accusations of our egotism and selfishness and self-absorption, seem to miss the mark. The actual texture of our daily activities is not well represented by most of the theories about us, whether voiced by friend or foe.

Equality

As for *fraternity*, so for *equality:* our theory is inferior to our practice. In every large society known to history, there have been elites and commoners, persons of great wealth and persons of poverty. Yet as Tocqueville noted in *Democracy in America* (1835), the idea of equality was sweeping the Western world in so uncritical a way that it threatened to overwhelm the idea of liberty. It is odd, indeed, that the specifically democratic and specifically capitalist ideal of equality has not been clearly delineated. In the socialist world, actual practice seems to be in inverse relation to theory.

There is no pretense of political equality between the ruling elites and ordinary populations in the Soviet Union or in China. Membership in the Communist party confers political privileges in which no others share. Against those in positions of power, there are no checks and balances. In the economic sphere, serious inequalities in the class structure of socialist nations deserve public study. There are many indications that, sheerly on the level of wealth and economic privilege, the gap between the top elites and the lowest ranking citizens is greater in socialist nations than in the United States. This is an empirical matter, subject to empirical observation; I submit it as no more than an hypothesis. My point is that reality does not often match what ideology preaches. The rare images one receives from closed societies do not suggest that all persons within them live under conditions of economic equality, or that economic mobility is as pervasive and open there as here.

The dynamism within a democratic capitalist system like our own originates in the conviction (1) that both elites and those at the economic bottom will circulate; and (2) that there is opportunity for all, whatever their starting place, not only to better their positions but also to go as far as imagination, work, and luck will take them. The system does not guarantee success. It does guarantee opportunity. It multiplies occasions for luck and good fortune. It is an open, porous, highly mobile system. Downward mobility is as characteristic of it as upward mobility. Just as neighborhoods decline and old plantation mansions fall into decay, so do individual families lose money and status. About half of all those in the top 20 percent by income in one generation will not be represented within it twenty years later, and the same holds true for the bottom 20 percent.

Our culture does not believe that individuals are of equal talent, motivation, drive, attitude, or aptitude. It does not hold that all have equal luck. Emphatically, it does not hold that all do, or should, achieve equal outcomes. It does hold that all have equal rights under the law, and that each should have an opportunity to improve his or her own station.

In one sense, our culture is committed to equality; in another it is committed to inequality. It holds that equal work should receive equal pay. It also holds that superior work should be rewarded with superior pay. It holds that every worker is entitled to a just wage. It also holds that some persons of rare talent (or rare value, in whatever marketable way) may receive rewards not so much commensurate with their work as with their gift and its desirability.

In the marketplace, our culture makes at least two judgments about persons of rare talent or rare value. On the one hand, people wish that rewards would be assigned for intrinsic value, so that rare talents will be recognized for their own sake and appropriately rewarded. There is discomfort when a movie star, athlete, winner of a lottery, or very highly paid corporate manager receives a reward seemingly far out of proportion to the person's intrinsic talent. On the other hand, there is at least a grudging respect for the marketplace, for changing tastes and opportunities, for the "lucky break"— Lana Turner "discovered" while sipping a soda. In an open and mobile society, few values are fixed. The role of luck has, therefore, long been celebrated in American popular culture. "Opportunity seldom knocks twice" is folk wisdom's counterpoise to belief in hard work alone: "Thank your lucky stars." The cultural system promises opportunity, but warns that it may be missed. It recommends hard work and self-improvement, so that when opportunity comes we will not be inadequately prepared to take advantage of it. And it recognizes a certain principle of absurdity in the working of the marketplace. The marketplace is not created by a set of rational planners. It results from the decisions of buyers and sellers. Its outcome is often counter-intuitive and even counter-rational in its workings. It operates at times like a lottery, and sometimes individuals, through neither merit nor fault of their own, win or lose big.

Since everyone has a chance in the lottery of life, everyone is equal; lotteries are no respecters of persons. Still, good luck and bad luck are not believed to be equally distributed. In our culture, rationalists—and egalitarians—frequently overlook the very large role of nonsystematic luck in human affairs. Yet, the distinction between receiving a superior reward for intrinsic reasons—for superior talent or superior performance—and receiving a superior reward because of demand in the marketplace is an important distinction. One can prefer a system of respect for intrinsic merit and yet respect the institution of the market, even when it does not reward intrinsic qualities in due proportion. In the best of all possible worlds, the market would reflect only intrinsic values. In the real world, the liberty given the market (for the sake of a greater good) permits it sometimes to issue forth in less than "rational" results.

The marketplace, then, does not and cannot reward everyone in a fully rational and appropriate way. The market is a harsh master. It is an instrument certain to bring about some serious inequalities. In order to defend democratic capitalism, one does not have to deny that the market system is, in this sense, nonrational. The reasons for supporting a market system are not absolutist but instrumental. The market works exceedingly well for certain purposes. And its chief purpose is to provide a device whereby the imagination and even the selfishness of individuals can be stimulated, on the one hand, and transmuted into a powerful instrument of social change, on the other. Those societies that adopted the market system became, in fact, the first modern societies. They provided the enormous "leap forward" that has transformed the face of the planet these last two hundred years.

Societies that have chosen other routes to modernity have not solved fundamental problems of political and economic equality. They are rigid, autocratic, even totalitarian. Indeed, any society based upon an agency of strong central planning, backed up by agencies of enforcement, cannot be democratic. The more democratic a nation is, the less "rational" its national planning must necessarily be. The more "rational" its planning, the less democratic it must necessarily be. For democracy works rather as a market does, by the pressures and counterpressures of many diverse interest groups, willing to compromise but seldom willing to yield entirely to someone else's vision of the rational.

Liberty

I have saved until last the discussion of liberty, for this theme is far more readily conceded by anticapitalist thinkers. Their way of getting around the point, however, is to make light of "bourgeois liberty" and "consumer freedom" and to appeal to some deeper spiritual, humanistic liberty. Thinkers of the left like Herbert Marcuse and thinkers of the right like Malcolm Muggeridge have both accused capitalist society in this way. But the trouble is that any society which would permit human beings a full and untrammeled liberty must also permit human beings—as God does (if one may make the point theologically)—to use their freedom for less than admirable purposes.

A democratic capitalist society does not promise salvation. It does not even promise the development of a higher human type (like the "new man" of socialist ideology). It does promise that each individual human being will have, by constitutional right and even by a certain minimal economic opportunity, freedom to think and to act, to aspire, to improve himself and his lot, and to move, go about, and make an almost unlimited series of choices about how to spend his or her life. The system does not promise that each person will, in fact, make out of himself or herself what he or she would like. But it does, in fact, give ample room for each person to experiment and to try. Most citizens, it appears, do in fact better their own lot over the course of their lifetimes. But not all do. In a perfectly free system, a realist would not expect all to succeed equally, nor each to avoid some measure of failure.

Even the poorest person in our society, except in the most remote locations, has access to books. A magnificent library of a hundred of the world's great classics might easily be purchased in paperback books, or consulted at free public libraries. Few who had the unconquerable desire to educate themselves would find it impossible to do so. An enormous amount of work, not least in the poorest areas of our cities and in rural areas, needs doing. Still, unemployment affects many, and millions of our citizens remain poor and psychologically hardly able to better their lot. To diagnose the causes of cultural despair in such remaining pockets of the population remains an unfinished order of business. But here the problem is to bring such persons *into* the system of personal liberties and personal responsibilities, rather than to devise some special system of dependence on their behalf. Some critics forget that the precise pathology inflicted upon many citizens was an enforced pattern of dependence, under conditions of slavery and segregation.

Another accusation against democratic capitalism is that it allows *too much liberty,* of a deceptive kind. The system, so runs this criticism, is so flexible that it "co-opts" its critics, absorbing their protests and their accusations, without undergoing revolutionary change. But this is, in fact, only an admission of the weakness of singleminded ideology. A free system, open and willing to listen to criticism and to learn from it, will gradually win over large numbers of its own internal critics. How can they not give their loyalty to a system that hears them out and changes as it goes? Few are the persons who expect a whole system to jump when they snap their fingers. And the notion that some "revolution" might make our society still freer than it is does not gain much plausibility from the history of other revolutions on this planet. A democratic capitalist society is committed to experimentation, to flexibility, and to change. The record shows that its economic, political, and cultural components have undergone immense changes, generation by generation.

Finally, the connection between the political system and the economic system—and between each of these and the cultural system—should be clearly perceived. More than any other system in history, our system nourishes—and amply rewards—its own critics. It does not demand that its citizens love or praise it. It encourages them to criticize it in each single part and in the whole. But this almost unprecedented capacity of a historical system to absorb and to benefit by internal criticism only maddens many of its critics. Like sons of a permissive father, they seek yet more wounding ways by which to make their presence felt. Intellectuals long to be taken seriously. Those whose sense of their own integrity obliges them to stand over against the system in which they live play an unprecedented historical role. For this reason, it is necessary not only to develop aggressive arguments about the actual texture of life in a democratic capitalist society, but also to try to understand the social situation from which its critics view it.

5

The New Class

Since World War II, great changes in the American social order have altered the domestic balance of power. Even a short time ago there would have been widespread agreement with Calvin Coolidge's sentiment, "the business of America is business." Since World War II, a new social class has emerged whose main business is not business. The fact that there is such a class—the intellectual class, or more exactly, the class whose power base lies in "the knowledge industry" and in the State—is not new. But two powerful changes have recently raised the status of that class: (1) it has grown enormously in numbers, both in its leadership cadres and in the millions of citizens whose cause is linked with theirs; and (2) simultaneously, powerful instruments of social change have emerged which are perfectly suited to its own needs and purposes. These are the national media of communication, especially television and radio, but also the national news magazines and the major national organs of daily news. These two changes have critically affected the nation's self-understanding. The "rules of the game" have been changed.

Not many decades ago, truly wealthy and powerful people preferred to avoid being in the news. "The news" was treated as a diversion, a vulgar entertainment, hardly as a carrier of real power. For the purposes of real power, many believed that "no news is good news." In 1960, the campaign of John F. Kennedy taught the new class the glamour of politics. Kennedy saw television, the news magazines, and the press as a source of power to be courted at least as assiduously as any other source. The political importance of the press had long been recognized, but Kennedy comprehended how thoroughly the various forms of media are interrelated and grasped the new access to national power made possible through television.

The existence of the new suburban "supermarket" vote—the vote of the bright, young, technically expert professionals produced by World War II and by the swift expansion of the educational system afterwards—was carefully exploited by "the new frontier."

Characteristics of the New Class

The emergence of any new class in history brings new expectations. A new class employs new instruments of power, manifests new interests, exemplifies new ambitions, and attempts to make the whole culture reflect its own tastes, ideals, and styles of living. All four of these characteristics are manifested by this new class. We have witnessed the growth of the "new politics" and "media politics"; a rising interest in "change," that is, the displacement of older centers of power; new types of self-aggrandizement through new legislation and new forms of litigation (since the new class often prefers to acquire power through the courts rather than through the legislatures); and a "new morality." The new elites have chosen as their center of power the communications industry—the New York–Los Angeles axis—and their main base of operations the suburban communities near major universities (such as the Boston suburbs, Madison, Evanston, Ann Arbor, and Berkeley). Some heroes of the new elites have been Dan Rather, Robert Redford, Barry Commoner, George McGovern, Tom Hayden, Andrew Young, Gloria Steinem, Hunter S. Thompson, Ralph Nader, and John Gardner. Their battle cries have often been "morality," "a caring society," and "sensitive caring individuals." They have often claimed to desire an alliance of "the poor, the black, the young, and women."

The new class is defined by income, education, and status. In numbers, we may sketch its dimensions in three steps. Almost 20 percent of all wage earners have incomes above $20,000 (about 5 percent above $25,000).[1] About 15 percent of all adults have had four years of college education. About 25 percent of all those in the work force have professional or managerial positions. In these terms, the new class overlaps older elites of the business community and the old politics, so a further distinction is needed. The center of power of the older leading class was business; that of the new class is the power of the State. This distinction only appears to overlap the older distinction between "liberals" and "conservatives." Con-

---

[1] U.S. Census Bureau, *Current Population Report*, "Money Income and Poverty Status of Families and Persons in U.S.: 1977," Series P60, no. 116, July 1978.

servatives have traditionally resisted State power. Liberals have, since 1935, chosen the power of the State, particularly that of the federal government, as their preferred instrument of "change." Characteristically, the statist wing of the new class has been activated by appeals to "get this country moving again," "leadership for a change," and the like. Still, there are many liberals who oppose the new class—senators like Jackson and Moynihan; representatives like Foley and O'Hara; intellectuals like Ben Wattenberg, Norman Podhoretz, and Irving Kristol. So the distinction between liberal and conservative is not sufficient.

From the point of view of their liberal critics, what distinguishes the left wing of the new class is its hidden agenda of self-aggrandizement, its adversarial posture against the central conceptions of our political, economic, and cultural systems, and its attempts to short-circuit the will of the majority (even of a majority within the Democratic party). The new class, so defined, is the carrier of the new politics, the new ideology, and the new morality. Not all its contributions have been negative. But, so its critics believe, its intellectual force is inimical to each of the three dimensions of our system. Paul Johnson describes its biases in a book aptly called *The Enemies of Society* (1977).

In his lucid and lyrical little book, *Sociology as an Art Form* (1976), Robert Nisbet lists some of the main concepts of the social sciences during the past century or more, concepts like *community, power, masses, progress, egalitarianism, anomie,* and *alienation.* In developing these concepts, the great social scientists have also developed "social portraits" of certain highly significant types of our era, such as the bourgeois, the worker, the bureaucrat. To these must now be added, he notes, the portrait of the intellectual. For the first time in history, a critical mass of persons has emerged who make their living by their wits. They are detached from the traditional institutions and common forms of life by our society. To some extent, this social type is a product of capitalism. It arose from and with the middle class. For generations, its numbers were relatively small.

At first, conservative thinkers like Edmund Burke believed that the new "political men of letters" were carriers of revolution against the traditional order because of their ties to the rising men of business and industry. They were, he believed, partially responsible for the incitements of the French Revolution. Such intellectuals lacked institutional responsibilities. They lacked organizational ties. Their dependence was, mainly, on themselves. Their social bonding arose from and depended upon their solitary reflection and choice; their loyalties originated in themselves. They were not part of the ordinary economic order of production and distribution.

The new class of intellectuals might be nationalists and patriots, but they might also hold to loyalties beyond those of the nation state. Observers noted that they sought passionately for causes to support and for forms of social bonding, as defenses against their own solitariness. From a sociological point of view, they manifested a certain instability and volatility. They received their signals not from institutional roles, nor from economic relationships, but from their own heads and hearts. In theory and often in practice, this social situation grounded an admirable and even necessary intellectual independence. It encouraged an adversarial stance toward all existing institutions and forms. It brought with it great insecurities and social uncertainties.

Businessmen critical of the intellectual class, recognizing its institutional independence, might speak with disdain of its "ivory tower" and discount its lack of realism. As long as the intellectual class was weak, its favorite self-images were those of the outsider, the stranger, the bohemian, the marginal but independent spirit. Allied to court or crown, as it sometimes was, this class might acquire significant social power. Dependent upon the marketability of its own books, paintings, writings, or music, it long knew significant poverty and often allied itself with the poor and the outcast. It rose to at least minor eminence in the bourgeois states, which, in general, patronized intellectuals and artists.

The Old and the New Elites

Since World War II, as we have seen, the numbers of those who properly belong to the new class and of those whose interests are allied with it have swollen enormously. The national media of communication have given to ideas and symbols—the chief products of this class—a wholly new social power. Virtually every department of industry and government has had need of the skills and talents of this class.

The strength of the business class lies in a certain practical hardheadedness ("meeting a payroll," "the bottom line"). But the strength of the new class lies in its abilities with words and group processes. The new class specializes in "communications." The growing power of communications—within industry and between industry and the larger public—has brought about an expanded and powerful role for the new class even within industry, but within virtually every other segment of society as well. Far from being marginal, the new class now finds itself at the center of power.

Here two distinctions are important. First, in purely demographic terms, the new class is divided. On one side stands an adversarial class, critical of the political, economic, and cultural system within which it works (this is the new class properly so called). On the other stand the defenders of our basic institutions, whether liberals or conservatives. One is uncertain about relative strengths, but a reasonable estimate is that about one-third of the new class is properly designated adversarial. In recent years, however, particularly in the communications media and the universities, this has been the dynamic, vocal, and pace-setting class. It has, with a success disproportionate to its numbers, defined the issues, established the public agenda, and symbolically placed other portions of society ("the silent majority") on the defensive. But there are now strong signs that the more traditional members of the new class, on both the conservative and the liberal sides, are learning to employ the political methods pioneered by the adversarial class and with comparable success. This counterattack has been designated in the media, with considerable distortion, "the new right."

A second distinction concerns the difference between a class and an elite. The highly educated trend-setters of an adversarial temper are properly called an elite. This idea-generating elite may be relatively small, but the class of those whose livelihood and careers depend in parallel fashion upon central government spending is substantial. There are millions of Americans whose interests and life choices are clearly tied to a program in harmony with that of the new elite. If seizing effective control of the bureaucracies of government is seen to be the latent, and often manifest, intention of the new class, it has a very large reservoir of political power to be mobilized in the millions of government workers; professors, teachers, and staff of educational institutions; social workers; and workers in those industries whose economic base depends upon large government spending. Implicit, then, in the relatively recent emergence of this substantial class of citizens is a major struggle to displace the business class from its heretofore central position in our society.

If the former president of General Motors, Charles Wilson, could assert in the 1950s that what's good for the country is good for GM and vice versa, one might plausibly summarize the agenda of the adversarial class in this way: "What's bad for business is good for the country and vice versa." The adversarial class—to add a few more strokes to its social portrait—has every reason to debunk the ideas, symbols, presuppositions, and institutions on which the power of the business class has long depended. The relative weakness of the business class in the field of ideas and symbols, as compared with the massive strength of the new class in precisely these areas, has significantly altered the power relationship between the two elites. In the sphere of culture (the sphere of ideas and symbols), to put it bluntly, the business elite has been taking a beating.

PART TWO

Strategies

6

A New Strategy

Reversing the Trend

In order to reverse the recent historical trend working against the business class and in favor of the new class, three steps must be taken. First, the sociological base of the new adversarial class must be clearly fixed in mind. The struggle is liable to be a long one. Second, the field of battle must be clearly reconnoitered. It is no longer enough to produce a superior product and to distribute it cheaply and efficiently. The new battleground is the field of public perception.

Third, the traditions of the business world in the task of directing public perception have glaring weaknesses, easily exploited by the adversarial class. The agenda of the new class consists in an aggressive attack upon many of the presuppositions on which the business class has been able to rely. Everything that can lead the public to distrust the basic institutions or traditional leadership of society is grist for the mill. The adversarial class has a vested interest in debunking not only the achievements but also the moral standing of its class antagonists. Since in the past it was able to rely upon a national consensus and a public defense of its own basic presuppositions, the business class could concentrate its efforts rather narrowly upon its own products and their benefits to consumers. Now, however, it is not the products themselves that are under attack but the system that produces them and the character and credibility of their producers. The attempts of the business class to reply to such charges in a traditional way—through advertisements in the public sphere and through speeches addressed, for the most part, to other representatives of industry—fail to reach their proper target. That target is a public whose perceptions are in large measure focused by the elite of the new class. To alter those perceptions, open intellectual debate is required. The business class is engaged, for the first time, in a profound and broad intellectual struggle. It has not, until now, been prepared for that sort of struggle.

Taking the Offensive

A serviceable intellectual strategy requires that the battle be carried to one's critics. One must not allow them to affect a moral, high-minded, and public-spirited posture, while seeming oneself to be answering their charges in the position of a defendant. Once this scenario has been established, the battle is already lost.

The new adversarial class also has its interests, ambitions, strategies, and tactics. It is not in the position of judge and jury. It is not above the battle. It does not have clean hands. To be sure, it has captured the sympathies of most reporters and commentators. The spokesmen of the media, who ought to be neutral, are succumbing to their own *hubris* as they feel the rush of sudden power into their hands. They imagine they have played a high moral role in the struggles over civil rights, the war in Vietnam, Watergate, consumerism, environmentalism, and other highly moral causes. Most of the personnel in the media, if we may judge by their manner as well as by what they say and do, seem to imagine themselves to be marching on the side of righteousness. This moral pretense needs to be punctured. For television, news magazines, and newspapers are lucrative businesses. The product they sell is news. Conflict makes good copy. The media have a hidden interest in the struggle between the new adversarial class and the business class. To this point, they have, by and large, reported the struggle from its most glamorous side, that of those who have taken up the offensive. The controlling image is that of Goliath—the huge "vested interests"—being stung by valiant, idealistic, courageous, isolated Davids, defending the "public."

In fact, however, there is at least as much suspicion and restlessness in the land concerning the new Davids as concerning the old Goliaths. Just below the level of consciousness, waiting to be elicited, is the perception that what is at stake is *not* the interests of the public but a contest between two powerful elites. Every step forward by the new adversarial class has brought new costs, new taxes, new laws, new rules. The new adversarial class is statist. It can easily become—it is already becoming—an oppressive class whose intrusions upon personal liberties chafe and anger, and whose costs to the public are already outrunning its benefits.

Although businessmen traditionally abhor conflict, this conflict has been thrust upon them. The business class gained power and status only through a prolonged class struggle against the strong central control over society exercised by monarchical and aristocratic rule. The new adversarial elite plays in our society a role analogous to that of the aristocrats in the feudal era. They now serve government bureaucracy as aristocrats once served the crown. The dynamic growth of modern societies—growth in all three spheres: the economy, the political order, and the culture—became possible only with the victory of the entrepreneurial class over the monarchy and the aristocracy. That growth can be arrested by the victory of new statist authorities.

It is essential, then, to define the rival clearly in the public mind. Good insights and enlightening values have been put forward by the new adversarial class, which the business class can make its own. But the public's attention must also be drawn to the many hidden interests of the new adversarial class in its costly assault upon the majority. Rule by bureaucracy is inevitably rule by a minority. Defenders of democratic capitalism must stress the social costs imposed upon citizens by the programs of the new class. Who are hit hardest by the minimum wage? Many black youngsters of the urban underclass do not yet have skills up to a level worth $3.50 an hour. (It was antiblack forces, trying to protect the white work force during the Depression, that first brought the minimum wage to passage.) The consumer pays for pollution control. The consumer pays for the higher taxes paid by and for employees. Critics alarmed by the growth of the State must keep harping on the role of taxes in boosting the prices of every product sold. Instead of attacking unions and higher wages, businessmen, too, would be well-advised to direct their polemic against the costs of taxes and government-mandated expenditures. The workers of America should not be conceded to the new class. They should be regarded as allies in the struggle against the new statists.

The line of attack should be based on a serious national program, centered in the strongholds of the new class, to articulate the interlocking presuppositions in our economic, political, and cultural system. The war of ideas must be carried into the media of communication and into the universities. Some practical difficulties in that line of attack must now be addressed.

7

The Name of the Game

It is in the cultural sphere, in the world of ideas, that democratic capitalism is suffering its greatest losses. Given the new media of communication developed since 1945, the balance of social power has been shifted away from businessmen and corporate executives toward the makers and communicators of culture. To right this balance, defenders of democratic capitalism require a new strategy and new techniques.

There are two strategic locations on which to concentrate: (1) the points of distribution of knowledge (the media of communication), and (2) the locations at which ideas and symbols are made. At both of these locations, much more can be done than is now being done, and what is at present being done can be done much more effectively. There are also some misperceptions to be swept away.

The Nature of the Competition

In an environment in which ideas and images are stronger than fundamental economic realities, the modern democratic capitalist finds himself fighting on an unprecedented battleground. In times past, a producer of goods and services could concentrate on the economic aspects of his task. In the new environment, a false report about a product or a service, given instantaneous mass coverage, can destroy the market for a good or a service, no matter how sound that good or service actually is. In addition, the class warfare presently being conducted between the business class and the class of symbol makers (the new class) gives to each seemingly economic confrontation a profound political meaning. The making of symbols is intimately tied to the task of "consciousness-raising" and "the mobilization of public opinion," usually in the service of making new laws and of extending the powers of the State. Ineluctably, the corporation is forced to divert an ever larger proportion of its resources to the hiring of lawyers (to interpret what the law permits it to do) and public affairs staffs (to counter systematic disinformation). The democratic capitalist is forced, willy-nilly, into the competition of ideas and symbols.

It is a war that the ordinary corporate executive has not been trained to fight. It is a war fought largely with the weapons, and according to the methods, of intellectuals. When scientists, or even pseudo-scientists, call a press conference and announce the results of some study or other, the media love their exciting "scare" stories. The public, accustomed to respecting scientists, may then avoid the product. They may do so even if the purported study is defective or plainly wrong. Worse, even controversy about a product can damage its good name fatally.

It is instructive to study the way in which the new class characteristically mounts a campaign. Usually, to launch a campaign against any product or service, activists depend upon a "position paper" prepared by some academic or activist "think tank" or "public-interest study group." Most activists have been trained by universities. Most habitually move from theory to action. They may pick their exact target for tactical reasons but, characteristically, their first step is to "research" it. When they announce the object of their attack, they usually circulate to the press a 40-page (or even 800-page) "position paper," full of technical and analytic detail, marshalled so as to make clear not only the entire ideological world-view from which they proceed but also a chain of argumentation showing potential social or individual damage caused by the product or service. They may point to issues of health or safety, say, or to issues of inequality. They make use of the tendency of the public to desire such basic values as health, safety, equality, or justice and try to show how the public's desire for such goals is frustrated by the good or service involved. They take the high ground of defending ultimate values and suggest that the producers or distributors of the good or service are motivated by higher profits.

Often, corporations—during the first stage of this class warfare, at least—have responded to such charges by embracing the goals of the activists. "We are for safety, health, equality, and justice, too," they say. The oil companies, for example, have tried to reply to attacks by environmentalists by announcing that, in effect, "We protect the environment, too." The game has been defined as holier-than-thou. The corporations accept the game.

They are, of course, at a disadvantage. For the players on the other side affect personal disinterest. They present themselves as committed, sincere individuals whose only purpose (they say and may even believe) is to defend "the public interest." Quite carefully, they do not say that their own industry—that of public-interest advocacy—is a magnificent provider of jobs, lecture fees, governmental positions, and public power. They do not say that they are seeking higher public status for themselves, carving out lucrative careers for themselves, earning their income from their own activism. By contrast, the corporations are obviously defending their own investments, behavior, and interests. One side seems disinterested, the other side seems interested. Given this fundamental imbalance in the actual structure of the present game, who will win and who will lose is rather clear.

The Issue of Costs

The issue is not really one of whether the corporations have, or lack, "credibility." Credibility is always comparative—compared with whom? In the moral sweepstakes, the pose of the public-interest advocate is his fundamental rhetorical strength. Until the new class is placed on the same moral level as the business class, the game will always be unequal.

It is not a plausible tactic for the corporate executive to attack the moral standing of the public-interest advocate directly. General Motors tried to do so against Ralph Nader; the effort backfired, as one might have predicted.

The tactics must not be personal, just as the attack by the new class on the business class is usually not personal. Executives are hardly ever singled out by name. They are treated as representatives of a class. They are attacked as "profit-mongers," or as "big business," or simply as "corporate executives" (faceless, anonymous, abstract sources of uncontrolled power). The game at present is built around a morality play. To change the structure of the game the corporate executive needs to find the moral weakness of the new class. The weakness is its own affluence. The corporate executive needs to raise the issues of cost, and to appeal to the public to decide. The corporation is in the business of serving a very large public. It is usually far closer to the public than is the public-interest advocate. Let it take the issue directly to the public. But what is the issue?

The issue is how much things cost—in money, in productivity, in jobs, in growth. Every "reform" advocated by the new class has costs in at least one—usually in all four—of these areas. The corporate executive should announce that his company is in the business of serving the public at the lowest possible cost. Every modification of his productive process carries costs with it. The public deserves to get what it desires, and to pay for it accordingly. Emission-control devices cost money. How much money? At what rate of cost-effectiveness? What is the consumer getting for his higher costs?

The oil companies, for example, despite their low public standing, are in a relatively good position. When we go to a supermarket and obtain the prices of anything packaged in gallons, we find that a gallon of milk costs $1.49; a gallon of pure spring water $1.02; a gallon of orange juice $1.89; a gallon of ginger ale $1.98; a gallon of beer $1.40 (prices vary by region and brand, of course). It is difficult to find anything in a supermarket that costs as little as a gallon of gasoline ($0.69). Even at this price, the oil companies can show that some 60 percent of this cost goes into the many taxes required to bring a gallon of gasoline to the public. They can show how the price of a barrel of crude oil is artificially rigged far above the free market price. The oil companies can also show how tiny is their own margin of profit per gallon, and what that margin of profit means as the cost of doing business in the future.

The point to hammer home has two aspects. (1) Business is interested in keeping costs down, to gain more customers at larger volume. (2) Public-interest advocates rank in the top 10 percent of the population in income. While they are interested in modifications that may improve the use of products in certain respects, they are among the least likely to feel the pinch of the higher costs involved.

Instead of announcing, "We're in the business of protecting the environment, too," the oil companies should be telling the truth: "It costs money to protect the environment. We know how to do that, and we're responsive to the will of the public. How much extra are you willing to pay? We can all have a lower-pollution environment, if we're willing to pay for it. There is only one final judge about whether to pay more for it, and one source of dollars to pay for it— the consumer. The consumer is the one who pays. There is no other source of income. You are the judge."

If the game concerns morality, the moralists will win. If the game concerns costs, the businessman will win. Changing the game is important, if the capital and the imagination of industry are not to be stifled before the great tasks of the next generation can be undertaken. One need not believe that business interests always determine wise policy, or that they should formulate every issue. But it is certain that, over the long run, checks and balances must be in working order. And it does seem that now, in the present and the near future, the greater threat to the common good does arise from the sudden and unbridled surge of power in the direction of those who would hobble the economic system, thwart majority will in the political system (through judicial and administrative rather than legislative activism), and attack the moral bases of the cultural system. In some future generation, the struggle may have a quite different shape, just as it has often had in the past. In the life of politics and cultures, ironies abound. Former allies become adversaries; former adversaries, allies. Practical wisdom is needed in each generation to discern where in the tripartite system—economic, political, and cultural—distortion is arising. Decisive action is needed to right the checks and balances.

8

The Strategy

How does one change the balances? It is important not to confuse three separate tasks: advertising, education, and the war of ideas.

The Three Tasks

• *Advertising* works best in identifying a specific need, in highlighting the specific advantage of a product, and in setting up a chain of associations in imagination, memory, and desire, aimed at prompting a specific action.

• *Education* is far more diffuse and unspecific. It differs from catechetical instruction; it opens up arguments and debates; it concentrates on the sharpening of a student's intellectual skills rather more than on the transmission of specific information or attitudes. It consists neither in indoctrination nor in the transmission of propaganda. The holder of a "chair in free enterprise studies," for example, is likely to acquire a detached, nonpropagandistic attitude toward free enterprise, and to succeed better in raising certain questions (not necessarily favorable to free enterprise) than in nourishing scholarly cadres committed to the free enterprise system. In any case, such a professor would represent only one voice among many.

• *The war of ideas* is scarcely addressed either through advertising or through education. The fundamental ideas and symbols which direct the attention and the energies of a civilization are "the climate" within which practical thinking and doing take effect. We judge whether people "have their feet on the ground" by whether they are in tune with these fundamental assumptions. Not very many persons question these assumptions. But to do so, in whole or in part, is to engage in the war of ideas. In each generation, the fundamental ideas and symbols of a civilization need to be rethought because of changes in the practical world, in the linguistic context, and in the climate of opinion itself. In this rethinking, spurious revision needs to be distinguished from genuine and creative revision. In the realm of advance speculation, it is difficult to discern who is correct— whose theories actually bear more creatively on the practical order. Here radical opinions can make fresh headway. Sometimes they do so for good, sometimes for ill. In the general confusion surrounding fundamental ideas, especially in times of turmoil (this may be a tautology, since "turmoil" may be defined as "confusion concerning fundamental ideas"), vigorous attacks on the prevailing tradition may be launched. Such attacks—and counterattacks—constitute the "war of ideas."

It is obvious that changes in fundamental values, symbols, ideals, and perceptions can greatly affect the business climate. Until recently, the climate of ideas and the business climate seemed to affect each other sympathetically. The universities trained creative workers; the media of communication served as carriers of the ideas of progress, novelty, and experiment, as well as of commercial advertising. Only as the new class has swollen in size and ambition has the climate of ideas become hostile to the business climate, and in a costly way. The business climate is now affected adversely by many changes in the climate of ideas.

The war of ideas in which the business community is caught cannot be addressed by advertising or by education. Advertising must ride with acceptable modes of discourse; rules of brevity forbid its being discursive. Education follows and does not lead the way. The war of ideas is, in large measure, carried on *outside* the university, or in the part of a professor's life conducted in public, outside the classroom. The war of ideas is carried out in journals and magazines, in papers and books, in lectures and debates, on "talk shows" and newscasts. It is true that the university often provides the platform for symposia, colloquia, public lectures, and debates. Yet only a small proportion of the ideas and symbols generated in a university setting reaches the symbol makers and policy makers who establish the public debate beyond the walls of the university. To a surprising extent, moreover, questions raised in the public debate outside the university inspire work within the university, rather than vice versa. When environmentalism became a *public* issue, then universities began to offer many more courses in environmental sciences, and student interest was aroused. This point is worth noting, because we are accustomed to thinking that the universities generate the ideas, which are then discovered by a larger public. Actually, the relation works both ways. Practical inventors and radical thinkers often stimulate the universities from outside.

The Stages of Activism

How do left-wing organizations and public-interest groups enter the war of ideas? Three stages are discernible in their activities.

They develop an ideology; they have a goal, which fits within a general world view. Basically, many see "capitalism" or "business" as obstacles to the sort of ideal society they wish to create. They are able to draw upon the reservoirs of antibourgeois, anticapitalist thinking and images that have remained very powerful in our culture for many generations, particularly in the arts, humanities, and the social sciences. They are politically minded, and believe in bringing about "change" through the political process. The advent of mass communications has enabled them to enter into the political process *without having to go through the people.* They do not build political machines. They do not develop large, popular organizations. They try to create a "movement," built around organizations of "committed activists." But the main function of such activists is to create theater—to dramatize the "movement" for the newspapers, radio, and television. Although they speak much about "organizing the people," in fact they only have to organize small numbers. Their world view consists of imagining themselves locked within a system they find corrupt, undemocratic, and inegalitarian. Hence, images of "guerrilla warfare" appeal to them, images of small "bands of brothers" picking their polemical targets carefully.

The second step in their activities consists in choosing a colorful, provocative target of opportunity. Criteria for such a target may include the following: it should stir deep emotions of fear, outrage, offended justice, or the like; it should be easy to dramatize for journalists; it should appeal to widely held values, so that as broad a coalition as possible may be mobilized around it; it should afford some objective evidence in the public realm about some issue that has already created a feeling of uneasiness in influential circles; and it should provide a case relatively easy to reduce to "moral" or "ethical" responses.

This last point is critical. Apart from the deep moral sense of the American people, it would be exceedingly difficult to arouse the public. Moral concern is the number one instrument in the hands of the activists.

The third step of the activists is to prepare a "study" or "position paper" so as to "inform" both their own ranks and the media. The function of this step is to give the activists a sense of intellectual superiority and moral status based on the prestige of enlightenment, to give legitimacy to their efforts, to generate controversy and argument. In addition, since their appeal is largely to those who already think of themselves as enlightened and who already desire to do the enlightened thing, the ritual of intellectual consideration is a *sine qua non* of intellectual warfare. Schematically, the process of activism goes like this:

IDEOLOGY: The business system is interested only in profits, at the expense of humane ideals and concrete living persons.

TACTIC: X may be useful for corporate purposes, but actually does harm to people and represents an inhumane ideal, and is here dramatized in that light.

AUTHORITY: Research paper Z demonstrates the background reasons for our tactic regarding X.

AIM: Diminish the power of the corporations concerning X, and increase our power over X.

Examples of this process at work readily come to mind: the Corvair, cigarette smoking, auto emissions and auto safety, saccharin, nuclear energy. Even a seemingly innocuous celebration like that of Sun Day, in support of solar energy, has as its main purpose an attack upon the "energy monopoly" of the large corporations. The undisputed assumption that because the sun is accessible to everyone solar energy can "liberate" each individual from economic dependence on "the corporations" was essential to the celebration.

The Role of the Media

There is a further important point to note. Public-interest activists have clearly grasped the structural laws of the media of communication. These laws run as follows.

• The media are in the business of selling "news." Activism is, in a sense, an industry for the manufacture of news.

• Because the media sell news, they have an occupational bias in favor of the new, the novel, the challenging, the attack. With respect to news, the defender is always at a disadvantage; the attacker has a great tactical advantage.

• The media work under severe constraints of space and position (newspapers) and air time (television and radio). Hence, the gate to making news is narrow, and in practical terms, the guardians of the gates are few. In every television market large enough to have three local channels, there are perhaps a dozen reporters who cover social-political news. Multiplying this number by seventy, the number of the top television markets, one finds a total of approximately 850 reporters. Indeed, if one includes only the reporters who can break a story on the national networks, the universe of significant contacts numbers hardly more than 30. The situation with respect to newspaper markets is not much different.

In other words, there is a universe of 2,000 or 3,000 persons in the field of journalism, print and electronic, who in large measure decide whether or not there is a "story." In practice, if a handful of them are reached on a national story, or even one with respect to a local story, a new and important barrage can be laid down, with political effect. Activists cultivate sympathetic journalists. Activists meet a journalistic need. They provide a service. They supply good copy. More than this, they often make a journalist feel that he or she has done a good deed, struck a blow for morality, released some juices of resentment against the world of established power.

Making news is a form of political power. The structure of the media make them vulnerable to a new form of political manipulation. Invented by the "left," this is a game that everyone can play. It can be used just as successfully by the "right." In this respect, two structural features of journalism are of special interest.

First, most reporters, particularly those on television, run the daily hazard of covering stories over a far broader range of fact than they can possibly master. They are deeply afraid of making errors that could make them seem naive. Just as public-interest activists can play upon their fears that they have "sold out" and are merely tools of their corporate employers or their corporate sponsors, so also can others play upon their fears that they are using unreliable, false, or naively founded information. The fear that they may be called to public account for mistakes that they have made is their Achilles' heel. Thus, corporations would be well advised to be ready with vigorous, clear, and public responses to false or misleading information. These responses should be public, so as to place the credibility of the reporter on the line. Journalists tend to have thin skins. It is surprising how seldom they are called to account.

Secondly, the media of communications are also corporate enterprises. They depend for their income on other corporations. But most of the commercials they air (or ads they run) are usually subversive of the disciplines, virtues, and values that make democratic capitalism possible. Many ads preach that desires should be instantaneously satisfied; many commend escapism; many reinforce modish ideas, symbols, and styles. One sometimes gains the impression that the advertising departments are working for the new class rather than for the business class.

Developing Corporate Strategy

The main conclusion to be drawn from reflection on the logic and the methods of the new class is that corporate executives need a polical strategy that step-by-step meets that of the new class. The first place of attack must be against the fundamental ideology, which proposes that business is inimical to humane values and to real people. It is wrong to be defensive here. It is true that one could reply: "Democratic capitalism is the first economic system in human history to care enough for working people to enable them to live as kings and queens used to live—to own their own private means of transportation, to have as much upward mobility as they or their children have the heart and the mind to pursue. . . ." But it is probably better to address the issue more clearly than that: "A new class of experts wants the public to pay more and more for everything. Every new government regulation adds new costs to our products. Consumers are already paying far more than they need to. Every time you buy product X, you are actually paying Y percent to government in various taxes, and only W percent to the workers and shareholders of the corporation." Without saying so, corporations should shift the grounds of public discussion toward the costs attached to new policies recommended by the new class. "Every time you buy a gallon of gasoline, you are paying N cents for pollution-control facilities in our plants."

Corporate executives, of course, have not been personally prepared to enter the lists in the war of ideas, nor are corporations established to function for that purpose. Most intellectuals (the usual fighters in wars of ideas) are accustomed to thinking of corporations as powerful enough to take care of themselves and are uneasy about supporting such large centers of power. Indeed, the moment corporations become explicitly political in replying to their adversaries (who clearly are political), one becomes uneasy that the conflict might escalate and go too far. Tacitly, American history encourages a kind of public separation between business and state. By mutual consent, both businessmen and political leaders have refrained from heightening any ideological warfare that might develop between them. And this is probably all to the good.

Thus, corporations probably need a new method of accomplishing a task that must be addressed, even though they cannot accomplish it themselves. Recall the procedures of the activists. For their "research papers" they regularly turn to an "independent" public-interest think tank or university study group. They receive their legitimation from outside their own ranks. In this way, they enter into the war of ideas, as it were, by proxy. Modern corporations need to recognize the new element of ideological warfare in their own business environment. They need to enlist university study groups and independent intellectual organizations of several sorts: (1) to set forth their own vision of the world, with its intellectual and moral underpinnings, and its own connections to what they are actually doing; and (2) to rebut the opposing ideologies and accusations launched by the new class.

Both of these tasks are important. One cannot take for granted that most peoples of the world, or even most Americans, understand and appreciate the ideals of democratic capitalism. Especially among "opinion leaders" in the new class, the climate of opinion seems rather more hostile to the business class than to statism in its many forms. Businessmen know that their daily work helps to produce a better world for more people; that the system in which they labor is humane in its ideals and, in comparison with other historical systems, beneficial to concrete individuals. On the other hand, the system works by a certain moral toughness, a studied abstraction from other considerations beyond economic considerations. So businessmen often feel vulnerable to accusations that their responses have not been "tender" enough. In addition, they have, more often than not, relied on justifications for the systems which they acquired experientially and almost unconsciously over a lifetime. To bring these justifications to articulation, particularly in a way designed to meet hostile attack, is no simple task.

The task before business leaders, political leaders, and humanists in the present generation, clearly, is to struggle creatively to bring about that articulation, in profound and original ways that will add to the common patrimony of free societies. Liberty is our culture's most cherished value. It does not defend itself. It must always be re-won anew. The new class has, perhaps unwittingly, brought us the great blessing of living in a generation that must, for its survival, think freshly and deeply and lastingly. The competition of classes, like the competition of ideas, is the healthy dynamism our society is designed to generate. All benefit by such competition.

Appendix

Democratic capitalism needs an intellectual rethinking, from top to bottom. It needs to be willing to fight openly against the many varieties of statism now so prominent in the world of ideas. Moreover, the present situation demands a new response from the *practitioners* of democratic capitalism, the corporations. There are at least five courses of action corporations might pursue.

1. Each major corporation should create an in-house study group of four or five scholars-in-residence who would be charged with thinking through the theoretical and practical implications of the corporation's public policy decisions over the next generation. There are many excellent young Ph.D.s and writers looking for such stimulating employment. In the past, young creative intellects on the left have rather easily found employment in the foundations, publications, and study groups of the left. Young intellectuals who would defend democratic capitalism have had far fewer effective outlets.

The tasks of these study groups would be two: defensive and purposive. First, they would monitor the sorts of arguments being marshalled by the statists against democratic capitalism and prepare factual and analytical rebuttals. The status of public discussion about nuclear energy, solar energy, pollution, and other matters would be carefully assessed. Sometimes public discussion is out of tune with facts; sometimes the whole discussion is skewed by false assumptions, points of view, or perceptions—mistakes of analytic vision. The in-house study groups would prepare materials suitable for affecting the public discussions and correcting its deficiencies.

This function is especially important because, in general, the public affairs staffs of the major corporations do not seem to understand their opponents with sufficient clarity or at sufficient depth.

55

Half the success of an intellectual struggle depends upon a clear understanding of one's opponent's position. At present, it often seems that the defenders of democratic capitalism and their opponents are talking past each other. The corporations seem to be talking to the converted. They do not reach the intellectual core of their opponents' positions. Although those opponents may be comparatively few in number, they are enormously influential over the communicators of ideas to the general public. If one attacks the issues at a sufficiently deep level, one might change this situation and make the public discussion two-sided.

The second task of these study groups would be to try to think ahead in an almost visionary way, trying to imagine what impact on public policy a major corporation ought to try to have over the next twenty years or so. They could suggest alternative public policy strategies. The premise here is that major corporations do now act as quasi-public political institutions; they do indeed affect public policy and profoundly affect the daily lives of all citizens. How might they do so more creatively and intelligently? In other words, corporations ought to seize some of the initiative in setting the terms of public policy debate in the future.

2. Each major corporation should also set up a small staff of issue-watchers and "firefighters." When public policy issues flare up in controversies that embroil the corporations, this issues staff should be prepared to develop immediate responses and follow-up. This staff should be separated from the study group mentioned above, so that the daily work load of the former study group is not taken up with day-to-day controversies. Corporations need intellectual workers both for long-term thinking and for short-term "firefighting." The two functions cannot be easily mixed. For similar reasons, a successful presidential candidate in a political campaign often organizes his staff along these lines. One group prepares itself for the long-range issues of governance and initiative. Another reacts to the contingencies and hazards of emerging controversies.

3. Each major corporation should try to build up a network of sympathetic intellectual workers in the region of its corporate headquarters or its major operations. These intellectuals would be identified from among the academics, lawyers, engineers, clergymen, and other professionals in each region. Regular seminars, lectures, and study groups would be formed, for the purpose of thinking through the public policy issues that affect the intellectual climate within which the corporation works. Professor Seymour Martin Lipset re-

ports in *The Chronicle of Higher Education* (January 16, 1978) that some 89 percent of university professors consider themselves friendly to democratic capitalism. These are not the academics usually heard from in the public press, perhaps, but they do form a very large pool of sympathetic inquirers whose independent investigations and conclusions may be of great value to the daily thinking of corporate executives on public policy issues. Corporations could, at relatively low cost, subsidize study groups on various important issues, hold public seminars, recruit writers for corporate publications, and develop mailing lists for an information network. Many professional people would no doubt welcome the opportunity to sharpen their own ideas and to offer their own thinking on issues of concern to the corporations and to the public.

These intellectual outreach programs would dovetail nicely with the in-house intellectual study groups and issues watchers. They would form an independent sounding board for corporate thinking. They would give expression to a new form of intellectual democracy: thinkers from various professions and specializations contributing to a fund of common wisdom.

The extent to which a modern capitalist system depends more upon creative *thinking* than upon either capital or labor is not as often noted as it ought to be. The efforts of corporations to create a public presence among intellectuals in its own spheres of influence might well create rewards not only in public policy planning but also in new ideas of economic significance.

4. Each major corporation should support a few independent study groups, think tanks, and research institutions of national prestige and significance. In the world of ideas as elsewhere, status counts for a great deal (for more than it ought). It should be true, although it often is not, that ideas count for their own sake. But busy journalists and public spokesmen, who do not have full intellectual mastery or time to acquire it, usually take the safer route of turning to prestigious centers of information and analysis. Since the world of public communications works on a national level, it is important to have several important national centers of intellectual work on behalf of democratic capitalism.

Major corporations would do well to support a new type of institution, although one with historical precedent, a "university without students." Such centers now provide endowed chairs, to guarantee intellectual independence on the part of the scholars concerned about public policy issues affecting democratic capitalism.

Such chairs might be designed to support studies in fields of long-range significance to each corporation: energy policy, oil, transportation, foreign affairs, economic-political systems, and others. Endowing such chairs at a strictly educational institution is intellectually less productive than endowing them at a public policy center. The latter centers have an intellectual-practical purpose, distinct from the purposes of education. It is true that some universities have developed schools or institutes that are, in effect, public policy centers, and that these are often highly successful. But the recent practice of endowing "chairs in free enterprise" at such centers seems to be far less effective than other alternatives, because the goals of education are not precisely those of engaging flat-out in the "war of ideas."

It would seem to be useful, over time, to develop four or five major national centers of public policy studies. Disagreement, diversity, and difference of perspective and purpose and function would be in the common interest. Yet it would be wise to build up such institutions one at a time, being sure to achieve excellence in each before multiplying entities too quickly. The goal, however, would be to establish several such institutions over the next generation.

The purpose of such institutions would be to create independent centers of high prestige for the intellectual investigation of the theory and practice of democratic capitalism, with emphasis upon long-range goals and the alternative strategies for reaching them.

It is especially important to think about the *cultural* life of democratic capitalism. In general, scholars in the humanities inherit an aristocratic bias at least in part inimical to bourgeois, capitalist culture; and scholars in the social sciences tend to have a strong statist, social-engineering bias. The result is that even though the *economic* theory of democratic capitalism is well developed, and even though the *political* theory of democratic capitalism is reasonably well developed, the *cultural* or *humanistic* theory lags very far behind. This is the source of that faintly (or even remarkably vivid) anticapitalist bias so pervasive in our school systems, especially at the university level. Serious attention on the part of corporations to the *humanistic* component of democratic capitalism is badly needed.

5. Each major corporation should carefully monitor the ideas and symbols implicit in its advertising campaigns. As noted above, most corporate advertising seems designed to strengthen the ideas and symbols of the anticapitalist class. It does so by appealing to modish ideas and styles, to escapism, and to values inimical to the

democratic-capitalist ethos. Some thinkers detect a structural defect in democratic capitalism; namely, that in its appeals to satisfying the desires of consumers, democratic capitalism undercuts its own ethos of discipline, hard work, the postponement of gratification, and the rest. But this defect arises in part simply from inadvertence, through an uncritical acceptance of the bohemian ethos of advertising departments. There the "swingers" easily take over, and their beloved images of the "swinging life" nicely support the cultural ambitions of the new class. Thus, ironically, corporations empower the ideology most hostile to their own interests by the advertising they themselves put out. (Consider the appeals of Pepsi Cola to "the Pepsi generation," the appeals of auto companies to "the Dodge revolution," the appeals of the oil and paper corporations to environmentalism, and others.)

It is necessary to be far more aware of the cultural implications of the words and symbols used in corporate advertising. The competition of ideas is often being conceded to their rival by corporations themselves.

6. Finally, each major corporation should begin to be far more critical of the kinds of ideas and symbols it is associating itself with through its sponsorship of television programs, grants to colleges and universities, and other similar public expenditures. The corporation should avoid even the appearance of censorship. Yet it should carefully consider whether its own activities strengthen, or weaken, the values, disciplines, and virtues on which democratic capitalism depends. No corporation has an obligation to hang itself with its own rope, which is the prognosis Joseph Schumpeter saw being far too easily fulfilled in his prescient study *Capitalism, Socialism, and Democracy* (1947). Democratic capitalists have too long been heedless of the cultural and political implications of the ideas, attitudes, and symbols they themselves have set before the public. It is not written in the stars that they should do so. Nothing predetermines that they should. At issue is only their own intelligence in grasping the depth of the cultural and political struggle in which they are engaged. Democratic capitalism cannot be supported by every form of human culture. It requires certain human commitments, skills, and attitudes. To undermine these is to destroy the economic and political system, as well.

There are many other matters that might be suggested. But perhaps enough has been put forth here as a beginning. The main point is to recognize that democratic capitalism is now engaged in a war of ideas. The methods and means for conducting such a war successfully can be clearly discerned—they are well known, even if seldom set forth in systematic form—and the resources for employing them wisely, democratically, and in an atmosphere of freedom and diversity are plainly available. The next step is to begin to make them operational.